POETICALLY UNAPOLOGETIC

NISHTHA GUPTA

To my mother,

Who constantly believed in me, and always supported me.

She inspires me artistically and has always encouraged me to meet my goals and

be successful in whatever I do.

All she has gone through and still have a smile on,

How she handles everything with ease.

Contents

Foreword

This book is entirely a collection of poetry. The story portrayed in all the poems is the work of the author's imagination. Any resemblance to actual persons, living or dead, events or localities is entirely coincidental.

"Poetically Unapologetic" is a book containing stories of love, loss, heartbreak, and unbreakable bonds. This book is written by Nishtha Gupta. These are poems about how life doesn't always work out the way we want it to, but we can still make it a great life if we're willing.

Acknowledgements

Writing a book is never easy. Writing Poetically Unapologetic was the furthest thing from simple. The stories are far too common and some of us may have faced these. Some of us have made better decisions. Some of us just got lucky and didn't have to face the consequences of our choices. This book wouldn't be possible without my amazing mom Nidhi Gupta. A huge thank you to my friends who supported me throughout and encouraged me to publish a book. Thank you to all the people who always encouraged me to write poems. Thank you to my teachers who helped me with my grammar. You guys rock. None of this would be possible without you, the reader. Thank you.

1. The love that died

the first raise of the sun,
reminds me of you,
it was all so fun,
but it has suddenly flew.
those fake scenarios I imagine,
that it all would've been so different,
the forever agreement which I signed,
but I guess you declined.
thinking about you all the time,
you gave me such a good vibe,
when the rain falls,
I guess you'll not be here with me,
all those colours you gave in my life
are now blurred to me.
the greenery of nature,
I thought you did nurture,
when the wind will blow,
I'll realise of our love that flew.
when the birds fly in the sky,
I'll realise that love between us has died.

2. Sick Lies.

"I see forever in your eyes"
how could I not realise that it was all lies?
you said I'm pretty and with you, I'll be alright
but I didn't know that your love would fly.
I can't get over you, I don't know why
why did you let our relationship ripe?
your voice had me butterflies,
why did we have to say goodbye?
we had such a vibe,
then why did you let our love die?

3. A father like you.

You were the one, who always supported me,
Either in my good or bad always loved me,
I loved you so much, I can never explain
A father-daughter relationship that could never be claimed.
From the starting, you showed affection,
It meant way too real though it was fake.
You cursed my mom and were to harsh
I was a kid to understand, what you really are.
I was blessed to have a father like you, but now the blessing gets vanished as new.
You always taught me not to betray others, so why did you betray us for real?
Now, I don't care if you'll come back or not,
'cause my mom will be with me and you'll not.

4. The Best People

I wanted to thank you
but I was unable to explain
what it is to have friends
who can help you to get over your pain
you guys always made me laugh to death
you all are seriously the best!
zoo and incorrigibles are just names
but because of them, we got so much fame
so let me raise a toast
to the people who roast the most
in the whooollleeeeee world
HOMIES❤?
getting friends like you is a blessing for me
but sometimes I really wanna kick y'all from a tree
shut up 'cause you'll never get rid of me
you guys are the biscuit of my tea
-I never thought I'd get a best friend but
instead, I got the best gang.

5. Dearest Mommy

"Always and forever"
You & I are the perfect examples to this quote
What all happened can't even get off my throat
He let our relationship ripe,
2 years ago we all were so happy & bright
But now his humanity has just died.
You could've left like others and enjoyed your life without my burden
But instead, you stayed with me without any hesitation
I love you to the moon & back
We made our life go back on track.
You are my mom and dad both
I will make you proud & I take on an oath
Everyone made mistakes but blamed you for it
I know they won't admit their mistakes a bit.
We're enough for each other
No one's so devotional as that of a mother.

6. I find a new home

The night you came close,
You looked at me like I took your breath away,
You wrapped me in your arms so tight,
Telling me "you're so sweet so nice"
Hug so tight, it could crush my bones,
Still, there wouldn't be a moment where I let go,
I made you shiver and comfort you,
You kissed my hand every time I sat beside you,
Still so close, no place for overthinking,
Was all of this real or was I just dreaming?
I felt nothing for you at that time,
But felt everything after,
You turned my sweet memory into a disaster,
You wanted to live those moments again,
Wanting me to come close to you again,
All you needed were cuddles and kisses,
I craved for those and would've reciprocated
But then you took one step back each day,
Till you were at bay,
Looking at you was how I ended my day,
Now all I see is my lifeless face.

Efforts turned into excuses,
And excuses into apologies,
Your manipulations defined my meek personality.
Your empathy for others you reserve,
Your understanding I didn't deserve,
You said "you'll give us a chance"
Then you denied it with all your might,
You turned my peace into sleepless nights.
You be the stone in a catapult for instance,
Resist my proximity
Then you say you can't go a long distance.
There were two of us in this,
But you were never present,
You made me lonely,
When you shouldn't.
So I carried the weight in one hand,
And wiped my tears with the other,
Moved my rainbow and left with a blank canvas,
Your silence ruined my perfect picture.
Now I keep myself away,
Locked in counting days,
Sad because of you but fine most days,
You made your mistakes a habit,
And I got used to it too,
But now I'm done waiting for you.
Your apologies as bad as you,
Your words were never true,

Now everyday I have the Monday Blues,
For choosing you.
You broke my heart too many times,
Days I couldn't survive,
But I'm rising above you to see the light.
Leaving you in darkness, what I once called home,
You found your light and left me alone,
Now it's my turn to mend my skin and bones,
Dilapidated, tired,
I find a new home.

7. All alone.

I am here in the dark
No one can hear me
I am tearing all apart
And still, nobody needs me.
They can see a smile on my face
But what about the pain?
I am all free, but feels like I'm in this small case,
In where I'm dropping my tears like rain.
They say i make everyone laugh,
But who is there when I cry?
I am starting to feel half,
Can't they just try?!
It feels like I've vanished from their heart,
But still living in the dark!
Sometimes it feels I'm the target and they're the dart,
Tired of crying like a dog's bark.

8. Lousy Street

Her love which frailed upon,
Under the covers of the guilt inborn,
her lousy eyes every dusk and dawn,
recalled that one night of her forlorn.
That lousy street of glorious night,
Faded upon with the presence of her sight,
Tall trees with branches in fright,
Gazed at the moon reflecting in her eyes sight.
Passed down a love spot in the dark,
When a street light shined at the park,
Cupid's couple had that strong spark,
Made her regret love and all of the blade's mark.
Wandered this night of dust and fiery,
Her next stop was the same cemetery,
The eerie graves of it made her childhood teary,
But her soul envies the deaths in the cemetery.
Carried upon with her pace at least,
She travelled back with a forlorn feast,
Having no clue if she was a beast,
And finally, her hopes completely vanished.

9. I know...

I know what love is,
When you can't smile in glee,
I know what trust is,
When you are so afraid to flee.
I know what love is,
It is indeed filled with insecurities,
I know what trust is,
When you are one of the lonelies.
I know what love is,
When you are dreaming of wilderness,
I know what trust is,
When your pain can't be confessed.
I know what love is,
Or you just hated me,
I know what trust is,
But i also knew you were not worthy.
This isn't love i knew this,
Just the story of us,
This isn't curse i knew this,
Just something worse than a curse.

10. Too Young

All of these relations,
My heart was trusted just once,
Every two hours of all the months,
I poured down my numb emotions.
Drooling over my happiness,
Every bit of tears I confessed,
To my love I found in a mess,
Or was I too young to be blessed.
Feelings of mine became this diary,
Arranged at the corner of a library,
Among the books of lovers and her fairy,
The diary was just unloved and contrary.
Forgive and forget was repeated again,
Hurt and smile was our little game,
I doubted me if I was ever sane,
Or I was too young to be in such pain.
Too young for melancholy nights,
Too young for such breakup fights,
Too young for starving diets,
I was too young to understand love at first sight....

11. Fake Friends

Kept all those things you gave me inside a cart,
Who knew that all of it would be so hard,
I loved you but realised you took me for granted,
Behind my back you always ranted.
I guess our friendship was always one sided,
You are such a big liar,
You played with my heart and set it up on fire,
You were my friend but only for your needs,
I wouldn't have been your friend if I knew your deeds,
You were always toxic to me, but I tried I tried,
But now our one sided bond has died,
I know you don't even care,
Even after everything I shared,
Thankyou for showing who you actually are,
Before it went too far,
You really ripped off my heart.

Printed by Libri Plureos GmbH in Hamburg, Germany